What Is It?

The Story of Manna in the Desert

We are grateful to the following team of authors for their contributions to *God Loves Me*, a Bible story program for young children. This Bible story, one of a series of fifty-two, was written by Patricia L. Nederveld, managing editor for CRC Publications. Suggestions for using this book were developed by Jesslyn DeBoer, a freelance author from Grand Rapids, Michigan. Yvonne Van Ee, an early childhood educator, served as project consultant and wrote *God Loves Me*, the program guide that accompanies this series of Bible storybooks.

Nederveld has served as a consultant to Title I early childhood programs in Colorado. She has extensive experience as a writer, teacher, and consultant for federally funded preschool, kindergarten, and early childhood programs in Colorado, Texas, Michigan, Florida, Missouri, and Washington, using the *High/Scope* Education Research Foundation curriculum. In addition to writing the *Bible Footprints* church curriculum for four- and five-year-olds, Nederveld edited the revised *Threes* curriculum and the first edition of preschool through second grade materials for the *LiFE* curriculum, all published by CRC Publications.

DeBoer has served as a church preschool leader and as coauthor of the preschool-kindergarten materials for the *LiFE* curriculum published by CRC Publications. She has also written K-6 science and health curriculum for Christian Schools International, Grand Rapids, Michigan, and inspirational gift books for Zondervan Publishing House.

Van Ee is a professor and early childhood program advisor in the Education Department at Calvin College, Grand Rapids, Michigan. She has served as curriculum author and consultant for Christian Schools International and wrote the original *Story Hour* organization manual and curriculum materials for fours and fives.

Photo on page 5: SuperStock; photo on page 20: Peter Cade/Tony Stone Images.

Library of Congress Cataloging-in-Publication Data

Nederveld, Patricia L., 1944-
    Safe at last: the story of manna in the desert/Patricia L. Nederveld.
       p. cm. — (God loves me; bk. 14)
    Summary: Retells the Bible story of how God fed his hungry people in the desert. Includes follow-up activities.
    ISBN 1-56212-283-5
    1. Manna—Juvenile literature 2. Bible stories, English—O.T. Exodus. 3. Bible games and puzzles. [1. Manna. 2. Bible stories—O.T.]
    I. Title. II. Series: Nederveld, Patricia L., 1944-   God loves me; bk. 14.
    BS1245.5.N43   1998
    222'.1209505—dc21

                                        97-32479
                                           CIP
                                         AC

10 9 8 7 6 5 4 3 2 1

What Is It?

The Story of Manna in the Desert

PATRICIA L. NEDERVELD

ILLUSTRATIONS BY PAUL STOUB

CRC Publications
Grand Rapids, Michigan

This is a story from God's book, the Bible.

It's for say name(s) of your child(ren).
It's for me too!

Exodus 16;
Numbers 11:7-8

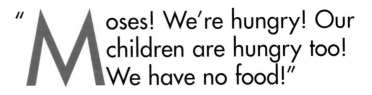

"Moses! We're hungry! Our children are hungry too! We have no food!"

God's people grumbled to Moses. "Where are you taking us? Why did you lead us into this desert? How will we find food out here?"

So many questions!

Moses couldn't answer all the questions from God's people. But God could! Moses prayed to God for help.

"Tell my people I'll send food for them," God promised.

"Go to sleep, everyone," said Moses. "Tomorrow our great God has promised to send food."

When morning came, God's people woke up and peeked outside. "What is it? What is it?" they asked each other.

"It's food from God for you!" said Moses.

"Let's taste it!" the people shouted to each other. And they gathered pots full of the new food from God. M-m-m-m! It tasted like sweet crackers.

Day after day God gave everyone this food called manna—and God's people were never hungry. Our God is so good!

wonder if you know that God gives us food too . . .

Dear God, you give us so many good things to eat and drink! Thank you for your goodness. Amen.

Suggestions for Follow-up

Opening

As you spend time together, look for opportunities to bring food into your play and conversation. Continually thank God for the good and tasty foods we enjoy and for giving us food when we are hungry.

Set out a basket of foods young children enjoy (bananas, apples, grapes, cheese, crackers). Talk about the shapes and colors of the good food God makes for us. Your little ones will likely want to taste the foods. To prevent choking, peel apples; cut grapes in half; and cut apples, bananas, and cheese in bite-size pieces. Pray a simple prayer of thanksgiving with the children.

Learning Through Play

Learning through play is the best way! The following activity suggestions are meant to help you provide props and experiences that will invite the children to play their way into the Scripture story and its simple truth. Try to provide plenty of time for the children to choose their own activities and to play individually. Use group activities sparingly—little ones learn most comfortably with a minimum of structure.

1. Provide pictures of fruit, vegetables, and other food items cut from grocery-store fliers. Lay out sheets of construction paper and glue sticks. Show your little ones how to make a collage of their favorite foods. Be sure to label each paper with the child's name. Suggest that children hang their collages on the refrigerator at home to remind them to thank God for their food each day.

2. Set up a housekeeping center with dishes, small plastic containers, and toy food models or dry nonsweetened cereal, raisins, and perhaps a few chocolate chips. Little ones enjoy acting out familiar mealtime routines and especially like to serve their tasty dishes to others. As you sample, praise their work, and thank God for the wonderful gift of food.

3. Set up a grocery store with empty orange or apple boxes for shelves, or arrange chairs and tables to form a store. Supply brown paper bags, empty food cartons, and a toy cash register if possible. Add wooden blocks or balls or other simple props, and let the children imagine a whole array of foods to choose from as they shop. Talk about the foods we eat for breakfast: the milk from cows, the bread from the bakery, the juice from oranges on trees. Stress that even though the farmer and baker help to make our food, our food is a gift from God.

4. Wooden puzzles with large, non-interlocking shapes are easy for young children to assemble. Set out puzzles with food-shaped pieces for the children to enjoy, and help them notice the colors and shapes of each food. Remind them that God made our beautiful world and the food we eat.

5. Texture play is another fun way to learn about food. Help children form pizzas, bananas, or

other food items from modeling clay or moistened sand. Or place dried beans and peas, rice, corn and other grains, and sunflower seeds in small plastic pails. Place the pails in shallow boxes to collect spills (banana boxes lined with plastic garbage bags work well). Provide small bags, plastic containers, spoons or small scoops, and a scale. Children will enjoy pouring and weighing the materials and pretending they are bringing food from the farmer's field or market. Talk about the helpers who prepare our food: the farmer, the baker, the cook. Praise God for all these good gifts.

Ahead of time, hide individually wrapped crackers around the room. Invite children to pretend they are Israelite children gathering manna. Provide simple costumes if you wish. Make sure each child finds at least one package of crackers. Enjoy a feast of thanksgiving as you talk about how happy the little children were when God sent them food.

You can make a simple matching game for your little ones. You will need index cards and markers or food stickers, or two copies of a grocery-store flier. On two cards, draw matching pictures of apples, bananas, hamburgers, a glass or carton of milk, and other simple food shapes. Or paste identical stickers or pictures of the same food item from the fliers on two cards. Make four or five matching pairs of cards. (You might want to laminate the cards to make them more durable and easy to wipe off.) To play, spread out all the cards, face up.

Ask the children to name the item on each card and to put the matching cards on top of each other. You may have to show the children how to do this, but they will quickly catch on.

Closing

Sing "God Is So Good" (Songs Section, *God Loves Me* program guide), and add these stanzas:

> *God gives me food . . .* (point up)
> *Thank you, dear God . . .* (fold hands)

Invite the children to join you in thanking God for our food. Mention some of the foods you've talked about in the activities and the manna God gave the Israelite children and their families. Or use the prayer on page 21, and have your little ones add, "Thank you, dear God."

At Home

As you shop for groceries, prepare food, and eat together, talk about God's goodness, and thank God for giving your family food to eat. Young children enjoy discovering where the food they eat comes from. Plan a family outing to a dairy or bakery or orchard. When you tell them that the farmer grows the wheat for flour from seeds or that cows and goats give people milk to drink, remember to praise God for giving us these good foods.

Old Testament Stories

Blue and Green and Purple Too! *The Story of God's Colorful World*

It's a Noisy Place! *The Story of the First Creatures*

Adam and Eve *The Story of the First Man and Woman*

Take Good Care of My World! *The Story of Adam and Eve in the Garden*

A Very Sad Day *The Story of Adam and Eve's Disobedience*

A Rainy, Rainy Day *The Story of Noah*

Count the Stars! *The Story of God's Promise to Abraham and Sarah*

A Girl Named Rebekah *The Story of God's Answer to Abraham*

Two Coats for Joseph *The Story of Young Joseph*

Plenty to Eat *The Story of Joseph and His Brothers*

Safe in a Basket *The Story of Baby Moses*

I'll Do It! *The Story of Moses and the Burning Bush*

Safe at Last! *The Story of Moses and the Red Sea*

What Is It? *The Story of Manna in the Desert*

A Tall Wall *The Story of Jericho*

A Baby for Hannah *The Story of an Answered Prayer*

Samuel! Samuel! *The Story of God's Call to Samuel*

Lions and Bears! *The Story of David the Shepherd Boy*

David and the Giant *The Story of David and Goliath*

A Little Jar of Oil *The Story of Elisha and the Widow*

One, Two, Three, Four, Five, Six, Seven! *The Story of Elisha and Naaman*

A Big Fish Story *The Story of Jonah*

Lions, Lions! *The Story of Daniel*

New Testament Stories

Jesus Is Born! *The Story of Christmas*

Good News! *The Story of the Shepherds*

An Amazing Star! *The Story of the Wise Men*

Waiting, Waiting, Waiting! *The Story of Simeon and Anna*

Who Is This Child? *The Story of Jesus in the Temple*

Follow Me! *The Story of Jesus and His Twelve Helpers*

The Greatest Gift *The Story of Jesus and the Woman at the Well*

A Father's Wish *The Story of Jesus and a Little Boy*

Just Believe! *The Story of Jesus and a Little Girl*

Get Up and Walk! *The Story of Jesus and a Man Who Couldn't Walk*

A Little Lunch *The Story of Jesus and a Hungry Crowd*

A Scary Storm *The Story of Jesus and a Stormy Sea*

Thank You, Jesus! *The Story of Jesus and One Thankful Man*

A Wonderful Sight! *The Story of Jesus and a Man Who Couldn't See*

A Better Thing to Do *The Story of Jesus and Mary and Martha*

A Lost Lamb *The Story of the Good Shepherd*

Come to Me! *The Story of Jesus and the Children*

Have a Great Day! *The Story of Jesus and Zacchaeus*

I Love You, Jesus! *The Story of Mary's Gift to Jesus*

Hosanna! *The Story of Palm Sunday*

The Best Day Ever! *The Story of Easter*

Goodbye—for Now *The Story of Jesus' Return to Heaven*

A Prayer for Peter *The Story of Peter in Prison*

Sad Day, Happy Day! *The Story of Peter ad Dorcas*

A New Friend *The Story of Paul's Conversion*

Over the Wall *The Story of Paul's Escape in a Basket*

A Song in the Night *The Story of Paul and Silas in Prison*

A Ride in the Night *The Story of Paul's Escape on Horseback*

The Shipwreck *The Story of Paul's Rescue at Sea*

Holiday Stories

Selected stories from the New Testament to help you celebrate the Christian year

Jesus Is Born! *The Story of Christmas*

Good News! *The Story of the Shepherds*

An Amazing Star! *The Story of the Wise Men*

Hosanna! *The Story of Palm Sunday*

The Best Day Ever! *The Story of Easter*

Goodbye—for Now *The Story of Jesus' Return to Heaven*

These fifty-two books are the heart of *God Loves Me*, a Bible story program designed for young children. Individual books (or the entire set) and the accompanying program guide *God Loves Me* are available from CRC Publication (1-800-333-8300).